BEYOND THE CLASSROOM

SCIENCE IN YOUR LIFE

by Charis Mather

BEARPORT PUBLISHING

Fusion Books, an imprint of Bearport Publishing by FlutterBee

Credits
All images are courtesy of Shutterstock.com, unless otherwise specified. With thanks to Getty Images, Thinkstock Photo, and iStockphoto. Cover, © Line By Line Vectors, Max kegfire, afotostock, Ground Picture, Beach Creatives, Ajay Shrivastava, FoxGrafy, Yevheniia Kolesnyk, Anatolir, Starlight-Studio, chuhastock, Rvector, Vadim Almiev. Throughout, © Line By Line Vectors, Ajay Shrivastava, PCH.Vector; 4–5, © Krakenimages.com, Ilike; 6–7, © Hakase_420, Connect Images - Legacy; 8–9, © Art Time 1337, stockpexel; 10–11, © Kikujiarm, PhotoByToR, H_Ko, SeventyFour, Ground Picture, Anatolir; 12–13, © MakroBetz, hlphoto, Claudio Rampinini, Cartoon D_Studio; 14–15, © yAOinLoVE/Adobestock, PeopleImages.com - Yuri A, 16–17, © Walther S, GT Stock, Ilya Bolotov, SBDIGIT/iStockphoto; 18–19, © Oksana Kuzmina, Drazen Zigic/iStockphoto; 20–21, © FamVeld, iMarzi/AdobeStock, christian vinces/AdobeStock, Nick Vorobey/AdobeStock; 22–23, © Simplylove, SUKJAI PHOTO, Jacob Lund, Nagy-Bagoly Arpad.

Bearport Publishing Company Product Development Team
Kayla Eggert, Theresa Emminizer, Kim Jones, Allison Juda, Cole Nelson, Naomi Reich, Steve Scheluchin, Tiana Tran

Library of Congress Cataloging-in-Publication Data is available at www.loc.gov or upon request from the publisher.

ISBN: 979-8-89577-610-0 (hardcover)
ISBN: 979-8-89577-698-8 (ebook)

For more information, write to Bearport Publishing, 3500 American Blvd W, Suite 150, Bloomington, MN 55431.
Printed in the United States of America.

CONTENTS

SCIENCE IS LIFE!

Have you ever sat in class and wondered . . .

If you have ever thought that about science, you may be surprised. Science is a big part of your life beyond the classroom.

In fact, it is a part of almost everything you do! Science is all about learning how the world works. We use science to understand why things happen the way they do.

The science of outer space is called astronomy (uh-STRAH-nuh-mee).

SCIENCE IN ACTION

How do we practice science? First, we ask a question. We guess the answer based on what we see and know. Then, we **experiment** to find out more. We gather information and think about it. Finally, we answer the question!

This set of steps is called the scientific method.

This is how all scientists find out about the world. As we ask more questions and find new answers, our understanding grows and changes.

How do plants grow? Make a guess based on what you see and know.

THINK LIKE A SCIENTIST

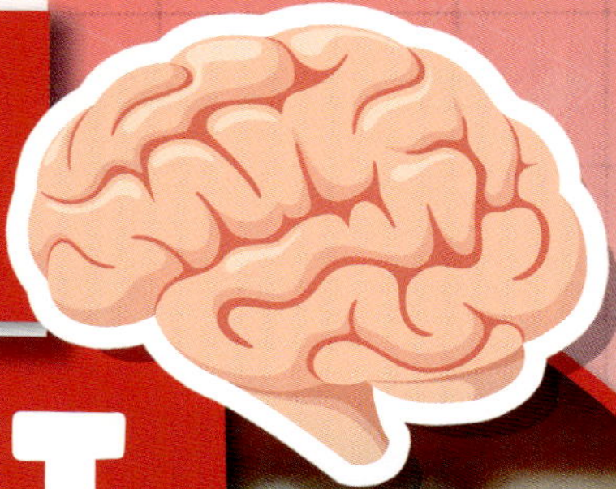

You can think like a scientist by thinking critically. That means carefully questioning what you know about something.

Critical thinking is an important life skill. It helps you make better choices. You can decide things for yourself rather than just following others.

SUPER SCIENCE EXPERTS

Science is an important part of many exciting jobs!

Electricians use science to help them power buildings.

Botanists (BOT-uh-nists) study plants.

Chemists make useful things, such as medicines.

PT doctors use their knowledge of the body to help people who have trouble moving.

Vets use science to help animals.

Having strong science skills is helpful no matter what job you do.

IN YOUR KITCHEN

Cooking is real-life science! Heating food and mixing **ingredients** are scientific **processes**. Heat changes food. Mixing ingredients leads to **reactions**.

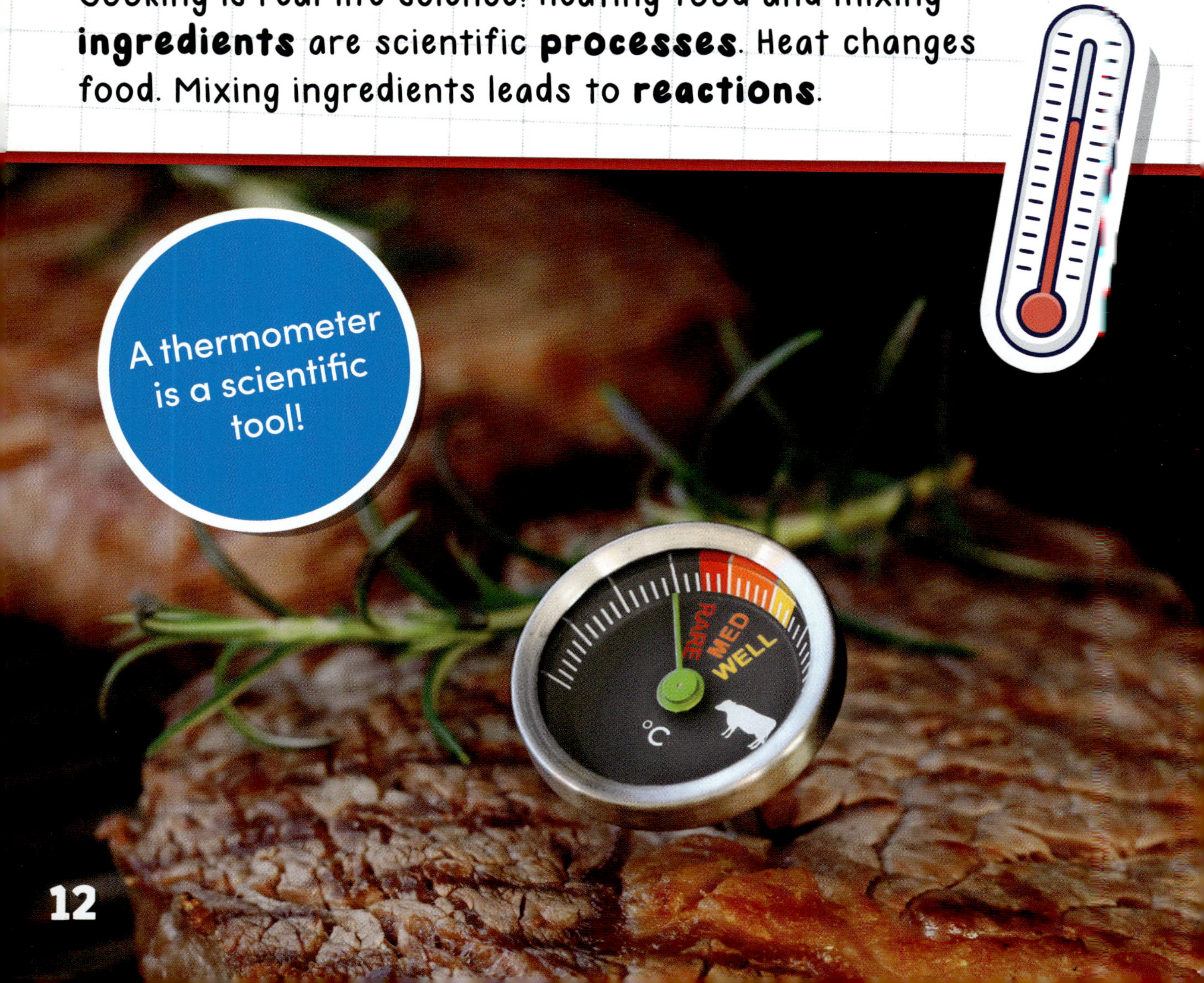

A thermometer is a scientific tool!

When we make bread, we create a reaction by mixing yeast and other ingredients. This makes bubbles of air. The bubbles help bread rise. That's science in action!

What kind of changes do you see when you make food?

IN YOUR BATHROOM

Did you know science happens in your bathroom? When you wash your hands, you make a **chemical** reaction happen! Soap uses a special mix of chemicals to get rid of oil and **germs** on your skin.

Can you think of other ways you keep yourself clean?

Like soap, toothpaste uses chemicals to clean away the little pieces of food and drink on your teeth. It keeps your teeth strong.

IN YOUR HOME

Plug it in! **Electricity** powers the lights, TVs, phones, and tools in our homes. When we use electronic **devices**, we are putting science into action.

Signs like this warn about electrical danger.

Since electricity is so powerful, it's important to use it carefully. If you touch an electrical wire it can shock you.

What are some ways you use electricity every day?

IN YOUR BODY

You can use science to help you take care of your body. It's important to know how your body works and what it needs to stay healthy and strong.

Nutrition (noo-TRISH-uhn) is the science of food and how it affects your body.

When you get sick, you go to a doctor. You may need to take medicine to help your body get well. That's using science, too!

Scientists are learning new ways to help people stay safe and healthy.

OUTSIDE

You can study science in your yard or at the park! Watch the plants and animals. See how they work together in all sorts of ways.

What do you see in your neighborhood?

Observing, or watching, is a big part of science. You can learn something new just by noticing what's happening around you.

PRACTICING SCIENCE

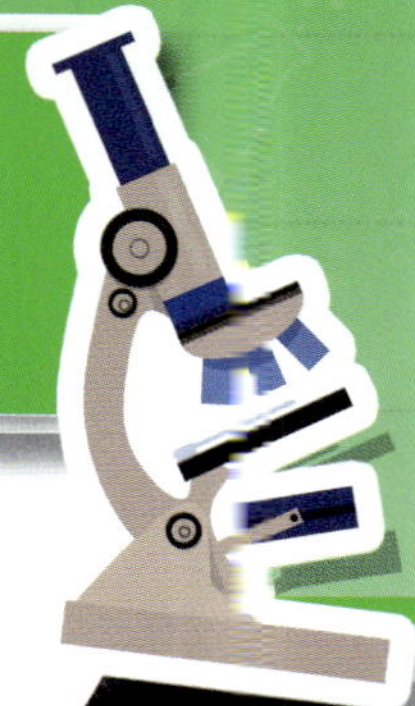

Science is part of our lives every day! It is in our yards, our homes, and even in our bodies. If you look around, you will see science everywhere.

? How will you use science today?

Look at the electricity in your home. Study plants and think about how they grow. Try out an experiment! Science can be so much fun.

GLOSSARY

chemical a natural substance that can affect how something works

devices machines or tools that do certain jobs

electricity a form of energy that powers devices

experiment to test how or why something works the way it does

germs tiny living things that can cause sickness

ingredients foods that are put together to make a dish

processes the series of steps that happen to get something done

reactions changes brought about by two or more things coming together

INDEX